MW00949567

The sad charm of twilight

Poems

Dan C David

Omar Khayyam

We'll never know what awaits us tomorrow.

You rejoice today; that's all that you have left.

Take the cup and lay you down under the Moon.

Because maybe tomorrow,

the moon will look in vain for you.

The sad charm
of twilight

Poems

Dan C David

ISBN

The Indies within

When reading Mr. Dan C David's prolific writing (sic!), you would suspect that he falsified his identity card, as no young writer could keep up with him, one of those few, who prioritize their opus, convinced that he had found his identity in writing, a fulfillment that comes beyond the ordinary meaning of things, from the divine that values the quality, the perennial, the expressiveness, and does not appreciate cheap scams. This means he is an influential author (his writing makes him compelling and does not need an official seal), uncompromising in his well-cultivated field of work, with high standards of understanding, judging, and interpreting literature, and happily transposed in poetry that differs from the questionable influences and cheap verbalism of the poetry commonly published today.

Dan C David can in no way be suspected of intentional evasion. In his work, undoubtedly, his opus is the man, and man is the opus. Even more so, his minimalist poems could be read as pages of a diary. A diary is a form of resistance in the fight against time, one of the favorite topics of our poet, which he addresses in Absent, the opening poem of this volume, using some admirable touches (one could think of the virtuosity of some pianists), which give it a memorable character, that drew my attention, for example:

"The time when I do nothing / I subtract it from the time of life, / I add it to the time of death. / And life decreases."; "

Honest accountant of eternity, / I will not try to falsify the books. /   I will smile, absent."

His relationship with this dimension is a tumultuous one, as is for any man for whom the accounting of wasted time in the first part of life, before finding meaning, becomes oppressive, generating heavy regrets.

As for Dan C David, I have no reservations in declaring that he shares with us the time of his mind, not pressured by clocks, hourglasses, pendulums, or other such instruments, devil's tools invented to show humans their insignificance, the smallness of their earthly life, followed paradoxically by the untouched, the unseen, the impossible. Thus death, with its unforgiving imminence, becomes a matter for which it is not worth the trouble to struggle to understand, credit, or discredit it in any way, minimizing its arrogant importance through detachment coming from the height of the superior self, where love in all its forms, is everything, for the one who knows the extent of his flight:

"You only / when you touch my chest / and threaten me / that you go on, / to think about death / it would be trivial, / it's not worth wasting my time. "

In „Dream" at the anniversary of a number of years that he is not shy to mention, the poet seems to have a less indifferent attitude towards this measure of all things and events, of existence at the end, seemingly more concessive, unless designed as a strategy designed to lull the vigilance and the abstract irreversibility of the phenomenon, as in a childish fight:

"His Highness, the time, has caught up with me. / he sits on my left shoulder/ near my heart/ and began to sing to me, / the same as always, / his songs. "

The poet's nostalgia is that of a return to his origins, to the purity of the grove adorned by morning dew, with the lazy sun strewn with storks and blackbirds, the nostalgia of a Transylvanian for whom Santa Monica is not a place of fulfillment in the autumn of life:

I dreamed of autumn in which the last worries / would be the corn to be picked, the vineyard to be turned, / the health of the children, the peace of the elders, / the weddings of the girls, / and the completion of the bridge over the misunderstandings/ of the year that goes down to sleep. "

Life is like a journey in which we only gather memories, which then magically transform towards the end and recreate themselves, some take on the appearance of miracle-working icons painted by unknown craftsmen, such as those that bring to our imagination the figures of our mothers and overturn the logic and the order of time, allowing us to become the children from decades ago, reliving that time with authentic happiness.

"When all will forget you, / and enemies and friends, / when you will become only a shadow / in the memories of those who will remain, / you are the cradle / to which I will want to return, / the nest in which I would like to die. / To descend into your arms of air, / to fall asleep in your arms of flowers. " (Mama 2).

Old age does not forgive anyone, none the children of yesterday, but it "does not come slowly, tormented, crawling among the years like a cat," but cleverly sneaks, like a cunning fox, appearing from behind the evening tree, making the reunion with a fairy of youth, now like a greedy butler with a huge thump, turn into a painful and lucid reality, foreign to the dreams of yesteryear:

7

"You saw me for a moment; / you passed on / as proud as ever. / Maybe you didn't recognize me; / I didn't care, I didn't feel sorry. / I looked at you for a long time through my expanded diopters. / I was sure, just like me, you forgot to count; (Clock time)

For Dan C David, poetry is part of his being; it is another organ, as vital as all the ones with anatomical functions, of which he cares for with the dedication and skill of divine a healer, not willing to compromise; so he writes for himself, as he feels, not for others, and even if he passes entirely unnoticed (not by the fault of the ocean that separates him from us) he attends to his unusual universe, made of most ordinary things, from facts of life invisible to the blindfolded eyes of his contemporaries, and the way he emphasizes all these elements is peculiar to the great creators of beauty. Because only they can reveal the novelty of the little things around us.

Dan C David, like any person of superior intelligence, also has humor, a quality he exerts with remarkable skill, through subtle touches, applied with the same style, well cleansed of tempting stylistic viruses. I feel as if I hear the words of some naughty Solomon from long ago. For a new reader of this poet, the simple reading of the titles of most of the poems could be misleading, because they sound playful and spectacular, while some have a humorous flavor.

What Will these be found at sea? The Parkinson's dead owl, Philosophy and mineral water, our love, a mess, Paraschiva sent me for a walk, etc. Returning to the recurring theme of Dan C David's poetry, I would like to quote from a poem (Past) of overwhelming expressiveness:

"Days, years, are no longer a measure; / it needs a miracle, / an abyss in which to fall, / in which to sink./ bird without a nest, / bear without a den, / serpent without a labyrinth, / alone in a world from which I cannot get out (...) All around me is gathering around my forehead / so like the space in an atom ready to explode, / to throw its sadness and longing, / to abandon them in the middle of the road, / in the footsteps of the past that has passed; / Old clothes, / torn clothes ... / past. His approach to the inexorability of time is, throughout the present volume, a detached one, of wisdom, reminding of Socrates' dialogue with the elder Kephalos in Book I of the Republic of Plato: „When we gather, (speaking of elders) most of us begin to mourn, missing the pleasures of youth, good wine, feasts, and the like, and becoming bitter at the thought of having lost so much (...) and that now, in fact, they do not live. I have met others who do not suffer. Nevertheless, in Dandavidian lyricism, love springs proudly from every poem, from every verse; it is the essence of human existence, it is an endless revelation, it is and is not a concept, it is, and it is not a feeling, it is the choice of the other (or the Other), it is, in the end, the divine, ecstatic love, like that of the Apostle Paul, who no longer lived his own life, but "the sovereignly precious life of the beloved," as St. Maximus says. Opening with a quatrain from Omar Khayam (about which Tudor Vianu said that "his work represents concentrated lyrical expression of its vision of the world") Dan David's new volume represents an extension of his opus, which I perceived as a daring expedition, of an overwhelming and painful beauty of shipmaster in search of the Indies full of fragrant spices, more precious than gold, and in search of the riches, he finally found waiting patiently within himself.

Mihail Soare June 2022

A book

To Dan

Simple love,
my love,
read on my face
the scribbled signs of the world,
burned by time,
by the waters of the sea,
slowly healed; not all...,
History, false stories
or disfigured truths,
both good and bad, of all things.
It's a book.
What you will not understand
keep in mind,
facts, words,
repeat them
until assimilation,
and only then
once and for all
you will know the lessons of life;
bitter and sweet.
Only then
you can close the book.
You are in control,
you can throw it away.

Alaska anthem

Silent stretches,
see of glass,
the scream of shivering of the cold eagle.
Crystal glass
collided with the teeth of a sleeping giant.
The ice forgot to cry,
thoughts turn white, cold,
indifferent to the crooked smile
of a reluctant sun.
The obedient light loses its fire,
goes into the ice, stays blue,
prisoner of strangled by time crystals.
Years are snowing quiet snows
one on top of the other,
burying the ancestors
in the white North cathedrals.
What do I carry in my soul?
How I came down and from where
in these places without yesterday?
The snow is falling, covers everything,
oblivion curtain
over the mind of an old man
who forgot to die.

Alpha Centauri

You were nothing but a dream.
Huge asteroid,
I was spinning around my axis.
The square of the mass
and the radical of space curvature
they were swaying on the shoulders
 of a white dwarf,
ready to throw me into the abyss.
You went down with the sign of the snake
stolen from the Sun.
You were stumbling with the heels
on the Milky Way.
I knew:
An inevitable catastrophe.
You will chain me
with your deadly passion,
you will attract me
in the orbit of celestial instincts.
I stopped at the crossroads.
The abyss was an undeniable prospect;
I jumped.
Freed from the fascination of your proximity,
I look at you detachedly,
lost in the abyss of all forgetfulness.
You were nothing but a dream.

An answer gap

When I think of you,
the old one,
behind the eyes,
in the background,
I see a meadow
which I wanted so much,
but I never got there.
Our moments rushed,
the years have come and gone,
eras have passed over the Earth.
We slept.
When we woke up
deserted all around;
a flock of questions,
an answer gap.
The spring of our lives
is gone.
The grass is no longer green,
flowers are gone.
I shout at them in vain.
Burning stones, sand, clouds of ash,
a thought like a fog and cold.
A flock of questions,
an answer gap.

Anniversary

It's not a beautiful day,
as we wished.
We heavily put on our shoes.
Half-frozen blanket,
the clouds descended upon our loins.
It does not matter;
we're not going for a walk today;
we're going out on the balcony.
We'll try to smile.
I fit your blue headscarf,
to hide the white of your threads;
I bought it for you at Herculaneum,
a long time ago.
We were waiting
to be announced our first child.
It has yellow and red roses
and leaves.
Oh, God,
how hard time passes now!
First video call
we lost it this morning;
we heard it too late.
"Oh dear, you look so great!
It was as if sixty and… years
hadn't passed over your lives."

Bastion

Do you see any sense in the mess
in which we cannot discern
friends among enemies?
I do not!
From the yard, we are abused by the hounds.
The left hand and part of the memory
were left between the jaws of the largest one.
So does your innocence.
When you'll stop
to look out the windows?
Gray eyelashes
cannot prevent cosmic radiation.
You will return to me abandoned.
The retinas of despair will be torn.
As so many times before,
you will ask me to be your white staff.
I will forget, forgive,
the wall around you
like a bastion, like a dungeon.
I will never abandon you!

Begging the clouds

The sky is not blue enough
to fade the darkness of the clouds
you look at.
Cold splashes descended on your eyes
at the moment I wanted to meet them,
beyond their depths.
They were turbid.
You put your palms to your ears.
Sparrows of the rain,
my words passed incomprehensible.
Then other drops came down
in your cold eyes
begging the clouds.

Beyond the horizon

The paths intersect
somewhere beyond the horizon,
in the past.
So far away!
Yellow quinces
bring me thinking of my grandma,
at her old chest of drawers;
She sold it one winter
to get rid of our hunger.
What if it is dust
and it stings my eyes,
and my shadow is more like a pain?
Ants sense the hurricane
and zigzag up on my legs.
There are no quinces on your path,
 are chestnuts.
We'll meet beyond the horizon,
in the shadow,
to tell each other
the stories we went through.
You are so far away!
You were a long time ago!

Broken mirror

The mirror broke
before you throw
the shoe in my image.
It would have been afraid
of your angry look,
of lightning flashing from your eyes
like a storm?
Through the scattered cracks
like the web of a mad spider
on the face of a blind wall,
the darkness of my soul could be seen,
and I was ashamed.
Crucified,
with my back to the silver
in which we once reflected
together, two angels,
and we laughed
at everyone and everything,
especially at ourselves,
I was hiding now
with a tense body,
the darkness of my soul
encrypted in shards at random.
I was ashamed.
Adam was left alone
under the apple tree of his sin.

Burning breath

When you move into a new house,
it does not matter how big,
you can't find room for junk.
You start to pick, to throw.
With the shoes with gnawed soles,
with dusty hats,
with the rusty toaster,
with bedside lamp,
fall into the trash of oblivion
so many memories:
Dreams lived,
others unfulfilled.
Part of your heart.
When you left,
with empty suitcases,
it hurt me the most
the ease with which you gave up
the pink pajamas with short sleeves.
At night, when you hugged me in your sleep,
I could feel your arms' skin, cold,
and your burning breath on my forehead.

By nightfall, there are more

Far, far away,
I see the deer at the edge of the lake.
She's not ashamed to raise her tail.
She looks at herself in amazement
in the mirror of water.
She has no idea who is following her.
But it does not matter;
until nightfall, there are more.
The quinces are slowly baking in the hay.
They have patience.
Until Christmas, there are a lot of days.
We're both looking, rummaging.
Have! she screamed like a cat pulled by a tail.
I had found a soft, warm quince.
But it does not matter;
until nightfall, there are more.
The lights on our street went out.
Somewhere at the Power Station,
a little wheel got broken.
We take a bath in the hot tub
where the turbines consume their last power.
We go out two steaming shadows.
A streak of fuel oil leaks between your breasts.
But it does not matter;
until nightfall, there are more.

Cherry wine

Do you remember when we drank cherry wine,
import from China?
"I got it from Maricica," you said.
You know, the blonde from the Party's Buffet,
and so on, you sad that Trajan is unconscious, a jerk."
"Drink in moderation!" you were telling me,
but you put the bottle in your mouth,
and as you were a little bit fat,
I couldn't see your Adam's apple
sliding back and forth, gurgling.
We couldn't love each other
because you start crying and kissing me hard,
and my mouth was filled with your salty tears.
I felt like a Kama-Sutra priest,
preacher of love without love,
of the total merger,
of crossing borders,
but he stumbles over the threshold
in front of his church.
You were falling asleep, exhausted.
I felt sorry for you.
You wanted more than you could do.
In the short sleep ship,
it was the only time
when your face got relaxed, beautiful,
white as a corolla of the Queen of the Night.
The empty bottle was grinning
on the abandoned table.

Cold metallic gloss label,
parrot ticket in Chinese,
looser at the destiny's lottery,
I couldn't understand.
Awake, you could barely open your eyes.
"Oh dear, I have to go;
buses no longer run
after midnight."

Circle

Your heart,
gentle hug
over the waves of sun anger
which can no longer fit
under the terror of impulses
from itself.
Your heart,
crown that caresses
hot forehead
and cools the sad soul.
Your heart,
a circle almost perfect.

Crows

We slide slowly,
we slip into a pit
in a world that doesn't seem to be ours.
There is silence all around,
and a contour less shadow.
From the cliff
the crows look at us suspiciously;
they seem to be rushing toward us
like in Hitchcock's movie.
For so long-standing,
your ankles are swollen,
to tear your sandals buried in the sand.
"Oh dear, how beautiful the sunset is!"
"But it's not evening yet; it's only noon!"
The ugly crows flew;
I don't know where.
Pretending to be a bride,
the ocean is praying in a whisper.

Did you read them?

If we could read the signs,
we wouldn't get lost.
If I knew how to read in your eyes
at first, like now,
I was no longer following you secretly,
like a shadow,
to count your steps
to hate the strangers, you talk to,
to wish him death
to the one who holds your hand.
You no longer recognize
the anonymous passer-by,
the man you once met.
You pass me carelessly
like a queen.
If we could read the signs .....
Did you read them?

Do you know?

So, we can sleep together
we should weave our dreams
in the net of a night spider,
to hang it in the corner of our hearts
where we will hide.
Otherwise,
what would I tell you
all night long
to keep you awake,
since you don't like
stories that end sadly.
But others, I don't know.
We will sleep together.
We won't get bored.
I promise!
We will welcome passers-by.
Good evening,
Good night,
Or good morning!
One day we will have to choose a name;
Do you know?

Doina Z

The first icon
which I was convinced
that God himself painted it,
was Doina Z.
I met her on high school admission.
There were three of us in one place that summer.
The heat was more scorching
than the fear and fever
from my soul.
In Zalău, on the way to the train station,
cobblestones were still in place,
and in front of Bordaş's blacksmith shop
the horses hid their heads up to the eyes
in the bags with oats,
behind the carts with stumbling wheels.
I've never seen Doina Z anymore.
She entered high school.
I went to Agriculture in Şimleu.

Dream

I was caught up by His Majesty Time.
He sat on my left shoulder,
next to the heart, with cold eyes.
He started singing to me,
the same as always,
his songs.
I negotiated hard.
Stingy, he stopped at eighty.
"But Your Majesty is not enough!"
Eternity intervened to soften it;
it was hard; it was as if it gave from himself.
- Ninety, okay?
I cannot more!
And, sullen, he let go.
Mercifully, Eternity fell to her knees:
"Take ten more from me, my lord."
Please give it to this mortal; it's not too much.
He will bring them back to another life.
I accepted.
Midnight came, then morning.
The dream fell apart with the fog.

Dreary through the storms of time

The sun goes down with arrows
among the first splashes.
They break into seven colors;
they mix again in your eyes.
Why just green?
"Let's run through the rain!"
The music of the drops screams in your voice.
We ran; the rain soaked us
and barely dried until evening.
The storm came at night.
We hid in a train station,
behind the lighted windows.
The morning came cold.
Desert around,
it was different,
it was no longer our place,
it was no longer your place.

It's not raining like that anymore,
once upon a time.
The sun is still setting
with his fiery arrows;
they also break into seven colors,
but I don't have any more
your eyes close to me
to fill me with green.
I'm still looking for you.

Elena of Troy

I crawl, I get up, I run, I fall again.
The turbulent waters come gurgling from the hill.
Is it a nightmare, a nightmare in a sick mind?
I climb to the top of the tree higher than the School.
You stayed in class, Elena of Troy.
The lady didn't get out either.
The frightened sparrows
climb the thin branches from above.
Below, the water rises and swirls.
Farther from the water, closer to the sky, couldn't be.
Yellow lightning envelops my tree.
In his poisoned light
I saw for the last time
your hand, outstretched, tense, Elena of Troy.
You've gone in an instant.
Where are the angels to escape you?
Where's Grandma's Good God?
The black angel of rain roared above the School
buried in the swirling, dirty waters,
he looked like the „Secretary.”
that grandmother had cursed: „ugly evil!”
He would come on Saturday night,
stop at the gate, threaten:
"Dude, if you don't sign by tomorrow, damn it!"
He was your father.
You never came to school again,
Elena of Troy!

End of parade

No matter how much I fly after you,
I can't catch you; I can't reach you.
The sky is so vast, so deep;
from time to time, I lose sight of you;
I can barely find you in the heights
by the smell of the perfume on your hat.
We are not storks; we are starlings.
In the morning, you enter the water with fear.
Wet feathers hang from your arms.
The starlings take a short break and fly.
At the station's speaker is given
fanfare music.
That's all the fliers need.
They leave the high and go down
to the nest, they left.
In the deadly heat, the hawk plunged.
He raised your hat; you got bald.
Desperate, you spread your wings towards me:
"Save me, darling!"
In the blue sky,
 a cloud of starlings
spirals in the gentle sunset light.
Fanfare ended its noisy program.
There was a deafening silence;
end of the parade.

Eyes only

From your cheek,
petal of a white-pink rose
another time,
the soft fluff is gone.
In the beard,
among the tortuous wrinkles,
from place to place a thick thread,
teasel on an abandoned field
in a dry summer.
Eyes only,
strewn with September sadness sky,
send me the same love
of another time.
Another love?

February at the museum

February, it's raining, it's cold
you can't spend the day in the park.
People flock to the museum.
They shook their umbrellas at the entrance.
Their eyes are filled with light;
as if entering the church.
In the garden, the camellias bend their corollas;
protects their pink petals.
Mrs. Figueroa pushes the frame,
and enters, trying hard.
It's Sunday; she couldn't miss up;
It's her day of visiting for years and years.
She takes off her crocheted hat and sighs.
Her hair flows over her shoulders
like a cloud of snow.
"Good morning, good day.
But it's raining; it's not kidding;
we will need a boat."
"Hello, Mrs. Figueroa, welcome.
You look better today than ever."
"Yes? Thanks. The bus dropped me in front. "
She enters the crowd scattered through the galleries.
She walks past the exhibits, silent as a ghost.
Reads the explanations labels; how many times!
Mrs. Figueroa stays up late;
she'll be the last visitor to get out tonight.

Fernando

„Como puedo consolar a un amigo a quien se le muere su padre?
Abrazando, abrazando, abrazando!" Nancy Degante.

Over the breath of the desert, under the killer sun,
the hooves of the wild horses shake the burnt stones;
a story that began a long time ago.
Thoughts fly over the barbed wire borders,
the fences of desolate courtyards
full of the bones of the unlucky.
Oh, Dad, stay away!
If I could stop the mountain
to roll over your bones,
I would run back and forth, riding on thoughts
from Orange County to Tenochtitlan.
The night wind would send me;
"Go, Fernando!"
But no, the cruel gods of the Maya ancestors
frowned out of the sad pyramids.
They handed down the sentence relentlessly:
Let the mountain roll over your bones.
You won't be able to hold your grandchildren
in your arms.
From the tree of life, a branch will be cut down.
You won't be able to sing a Corrido
to your daughter-in-law at the wedding.
Her warm arms and calming breath
will push the pain out of my soul
to dry it up, perish, and forget.

Final payments

Who will forgive my mistakes
when will I be leaving?
Whom the redemptions will I pay?
You can't get out of the casino
indebted.
It pays dry.
Pockets, soul, must get empty,
memories melt away,
icicles in the cold, from beyond, light.
Only then do the gates open.
Who else still has power,
forgiven, redeemed,
can leave;
a skeleton without self,
a shadow.
Where?

For you, I'm just a word

I am the sonnet murmured by the wind.
My heart is overwhelmed by you,
I'm just a word,
a name like flowers in a bouquet,
from the monastery, the last saint.
My heart is overwhelmed by you.
I am the sonnet murmured by the wind.

What music could tell you
what my self couldn't sing to you?
From the temple, I'll give you the best organ,
all the forests will tremble in the storm,
the all-night guards will weep for it,
I'll call cherubims from the moon
on Earth with their golden hymns.

Once upon a time, who knows when,
you will look down at me,
you will understand the signs,
your gentle smile will disappear,
you may cry, finding out too late
that my entire heart is full only of you.
I am the sonnet whispered by the wind.

Forbidden love

I couldn't touch you
even if I wanted you so much,
even if your gaze hurt me,
even if my helplessness
to bring you into my world tormented me.
It doesn't suit you; it's not enough for you.
I tried to break the chains around you
and the stone in which secrets were locked.
I woke up from a dream with the codes deciphered.
You secretly whispered them to me through a flame
which then extinguished.
I took revenge for eras of loneliness.
The darkness turned into a lump, into a point, into nothing.
I had been chasing you for so many years!
In a prayer
I had asked to have you, if only for a moment.
Greedy, shameless,
I wanted to keep you forever,
to hide you in my darkness.
To punish me
God took you from me, my muse, forbidden love.

Fourth of July

We went up the block to see the fireworks.
The day ends with unforgettable images.
On the neighboring blocks of flats,
the children are chirping,
screams at every whimper:
"Fourth of July, the fourth of July!"
A little sad, we hold hands.
Ours, at their homes with their children,
quell and scream at every shriek:
"Fourth of July, the fourth of July!"
Multicolored crown on the black oceanfront,
the West bank seems to be burning
more and more spectacular.
From the clear sky,
suddenly, gray leaves descend:
from a long time ago,
from afar, almost forgotten,
memories of a gray August 23rd.
We are not talking;
we look at each other for a minute.
You no longer have those eyes from then on,
the fire in them
Around ten o'clock,
we went down to call the children,
at their homes, each.
"Grandpa, you know, it's the fourth of July!"

From under the soles of our sandals

Late in the evening, on our walks,
we trampled acacia flowers,
asleep on the sidewalk.
It was like a peasant carpet
white, green, gray.
The cry
from under the soles of sandals,
only you could hear:
"Good man, good man, a drop of pity!"
"Nonsense!" I told you,
deaf as a cloud in November,
rain carrier only,
no lightning, no thunders, insensitive.
After you left
without saying a word to me,
I felt it too
from under the soles of sandals,
from the ground,
a living groan.
I ran after you.
"I feel it, I feel it,
stay,
let me tell you!"
It was too late.

Grandma

In the mountains with you
in the morning by the river;
You took water with a pitcher
and pour it in my fist.
It was cold; it woke me up.
I was throwing it back into the river.
You were holding the towel on your shoulder,
soap in the palm of your hand.
Through the roof of the hut, I could see the sky;
you always said that heaven is in us.
  "You go somewhere,
do not languish in the house all day,
as if you were lame!"
your mother told us
Friday night at dinner.
It was our first "expulsion from Heaven."
We went to Geoagiu.
We were back in a week,
hungry, tired.
Yore, do you remember?
It's spring now; today is Flower Sunday.
At Easter, we'll baptize Florin.
"Grandma" measures us with forgiving eyes:
"Hey, don't be like cats anymore!
You are big now."
God looks at us through her little eyes.

Gypsy
For Cecilia Voloch

You told me: boy, you smell like oak.
When I approach you,
my nostrils are filled with the perfume of beech nut,
with the essence of the beams from grandpa's house,
or from the little old church on the hill.
You get something; you use some balm,
any secret drink?
I'm not answering you; I smile carelessly.
I know the truth from my dreams,
from grandma's stories guessing in the shell
the events of the days to come,
from the heavy smoke of the fire smoldering in the logs
in front of our night tents,
from the squeak of the axles of the carts
on the endless road through which we broke
of the lands of the ancestors,
from the trembling of the oak branches
on our carts' dark covers.
Among their leaves, my sleepless eyes were dreaming,
looking at the deep sky.
I won't answer you,
I'll leave you with the scent of beech nut,
of the beams of old houses,
as in a cloud in whose mysteries
I want to hide.

Heavy sadness

Simion Puşcaş

The hardest part is when I'm sad.
You can't even imagine
how cold it was then
in my brain, in my heart,
to the knees.
I'm cold on my toes, too.
I feel like I want to wear
my grandfather's shoes and clothes.
I see him in my mind even now,
smoking "tobacco" from a pipe,
sick, sitting on the doorstep of the stable
next to his cattle.
He forgets about his many years,
about his pains,
he was looking at me with wet eyes,
with a warm, slow, soft smile;
He seemed happier than his nephew,
wandering with elsewhere thoughts.

Horses with red hooves

Behind the poplars,
to an obscure destiny,
run horses with red hooves,
swaying in the wind poppies.
In the red sun
escaping undecided,
red hooves catch fire;
jumping torches
above the thirsty grass.
Like two badgers caught in a crime,
we raise our heads at once
and then we dive deeper
in the dry grass.
- Are these the devils?
- No, they're the Cossacks!
Darkness clings to our locks.
A scary month,
yellowish crumb,
grows sighing.
"Where are the horses with red hooves,
poppies swaying in the wind?"
"They went galloping!"

I don't want to play anymore!
(Country song)

I want to come back.
I don't have anymore
the suitcase I left with.
I also threw away
my goatskin bumpy shoes,
bought in a courtyard marketplace.
Of all, only the photograph
from the sea remained.
The dolphin
had splashed your white dress.
You laughed at him;
you looked desperately at me.
Do you remember?
You forgave him.
Forgive me if you can.
I want to come back.
I love you.
I don't want to play anymore.

I don't care!

I can't love anymore.
I became a dry branch
that doesn't care about itself,
about leaves or roots.
I don't care!
The moon's forehead is too wide
and a little out of senses.
The sun is duplicitous;
you can't trust it;
when you need it, it disappears.
The earth, a senseless boulder.
Humanity, a crazy herd.
The fourth dimension,
that without precise coordinates,
extended geometric place
where do you live,
the garden where my love
was nourished from a lie,
became a desert.
I can't love anymore.
I don't care!

I feel you that you feel like me.

It's hard to come back,
especially in the rain in autumn.
Forget the reasons you left.
Now the return
it's just a question mark.
If it hadn't rained
for three days in a row,
you would have had time to call me,
at least one night
to look each other in the eye,
to talk,
as so many times before,
to a candle,
to ask me how it was without you.
But it has been raining for three days.
The cold drops
kept your thoughts hibernating.
Heavy clouds spread over the world,
and we are alone, desolate,
thinking of each other.
I feel you that you feel like me.

I'm dreaming of a different kind of fall.

September sleeps in my blood.
With his grapes, with ripe pears.
Far away behind the clouds,
the winter army is preparing to storm.
In the world, the leaves are shaking,
bad events happen;
more and more cars collide;
they throw us flying through the windows.
Asphalt gets quiet,
palms over his gray cheek.
Somewhere in the mountains defying the sky,
soldiers die wondering why, for whom.
The punishments do not take long to come down.
Burn our forests, our houses,
waters flood our expectations, our dreams,
with dirty mud.
I dream of an autumn in which the last worries
to be the corn harvest, the wine to turn,
children's health, the elderly's peace,
girls' weddings,
and ending the bridge
over the misunderstandings
of the year descending to sleep.

I'm hoping like a frog.

I want to fly, but I can't;
I hope I'm a frog.
Something keeps me grounded.
I'd do better in the water
if I'd tell that the swim is fly.
I'd like to know how the light looks
from the tops of the fir trees,
to shout up from above
to those who grow wrinkles
on the face of the planet,
and they make it weep and suffocate.
People I didn't love, I didn't hate.
I looked for them in the mists and ravines
qualities I did not see.
Eh ... but if I could fly,
to get out of the puddle,
to be an eagle, not just a frog,
it would be something else!

I rise from the sand

I rise from the sand like a worm;
so that I can see if it is set.
My job is to count the threads
yellow, crystal clear,
to interview them.
We used to buy fish
from the boys on the pier,
I fried them on the beach
in the evening.
Our fire could be seen
right from the lighthouse!
The dogs came after the alluring smell.
But that was a long time ago.
You are no longer with me.
Lying on the sand
like a worm under a bored sun,
I get up to see if it is set.
Yellow crystal clear
threads told me about you.
I go up from the sand.

I will smile at you

You're trying to hide back
in the folds of foreign names,
behind masks.
They don't suit you,
they have heavy mascara eyes,
grotesquely made-up faces,
they don't have your colors,
they are false.
Roads' dust
and landslides on the life's ravines
are encrusted around your lips.
You're a ghost
that I can no longer recognize.
Get out of the shadows;
stay in the light among the living!
Time, the river of forgiveness,
will clean you up.
I'll see you from afar.
I will smile at you.

Insidious memories

No matter how hard I try,
I can't break by my memories.
They sneak insidiously into my dreams,
they come from nowhere
in the minutes of meditation.
No matter how hard I try,
I can't get rid of them.
You show up in the fog, too,
but disappear in a hurry,
like steam from a cup of coffee
at the Mimoza Day Bar then,
one afternoon.
We didn't talk;
we almost didn't look at each other.
I assumed what you wanted to tell me,
 and you couldn't.
I remember now; I can't stop a smile;
You gave me my first lessons
in transcendental meditation techniques.
You disappeared like a ghost then.
We've never met after that.
Life, beautiful, ugly, inflexible, unforgiving,
slipped brutally between us.
Now you appear in my dreams,
sometimes in the morning minutes.
Insidious memories which I can't break.

Irregular clocks

I thought old age was coming slowly,
tormented,
crawling through the years like a cat,
but no;
Cunning fox comes lying, sneaking.
I saw you again,
beyond the oblivion's tree,
as if you had emerged from a foreign dream,
which I never dreamed of;
it wasn't my dream.
Your blouse slipped sadly
from your overwhelmed shoulders.
Cleavage, once gossipy,
had nothing to hide;
he had drowned unconsciously with time.
You didn't realize, I think;
you forgot to beat it.
The high heels
I didn't feel comfortable either,
at the right place, at the right time;
they struggled to smile,
but the smile was false.
You saw me for a moment;
you moved on as proud as ever.
Maybe you didn't recognize me;
I didn't care; I wasn't sorry.
Leaning on my cane,
I looked long at you
through my expanded diopters.
I was sure,

just like me,
you forgot to count,
and your watches too,
have been disturbed.

It's just a profession

To bring you closer
I focused my telescopes
at maximum resolution.
I was like Sir Halley, confused,
following the comet of the same name
which at that time was called differently;
he had not yet fallen in love with her.
You can't even imagine
how many arcs of a circle do your thighs run
through my field of vision
and as a fact,
you fall every time
in the arms of that skinny
with his nose like a parrot's beak.
High topics of our discussions
are relegated to the background,
the poems I write to you
late every night,
only inspire you there on stage.
I thought you were living them like in real life!
But for you, it's all a profession, carnival.
A cloud of love had begun at me.
I was like that, confused Sir Halley
after discovering his comet
and fell in love with her thin tail.

It would simplify everything

Well, if I could get your attention in any way,
it would all simplify.
It's night now.
I'm sure you sleep like a dove
in whose dreams there is no place
for sparrows like me!
Rare trams rumble on the bridge.
At this time, they are empty.
I'm sleepy, but I can't sleep.
I never went to the barber
from Christmas.
Maybe with the mustache and a beard ......
I hope.
The two lost exams I don't care about.
In the worst case
I'll take care of them in the fall.
It wouldn't be too bad.
I will meet you again,
even alone, maybe.
I could get your attention in some way.
Maybe with the mustache and a beard ......
I hope,
it will all simplify.

Jellyfish in love

With one hand, I hold my shirt
full of grapes,
with the other, I shake your hand,
so I don't lose you.
From the hill, the guardian is preparing to shoot.
"Let's run to the West;
we melt into rays; he won't see us.
It's like going into the sun."
You don't even seem to be afraid!
My mother warned us this morning:
"Don't go stealing in vineyard, children;
Today is a holiday; it would be a mortal sin.
Boy, mind you, you are the greatest."
At least you have an excuse; you are smaller
and the angel I love.
You have a poisoned spell in your eyes.
I do everything you say.
But I?
As long as a rod, with a little mind,
I swing around you
like a jellyfish in love.

Just as I get closer to you

Just as I get closer to you
by air, on waves,
my life is changing,
it becomes something else.
It's like an egg
submerged in boiling water.
Something shakes me,
like touching a high voltage cable,
as if my head were going in
in a microwave,
like an alien with glass limbs
hags me.
Just as I get closer to you,
I know it's you,
no need to touch you,
to smell you, to see you.
Just as I get closer to you.

Late spring

Even a lie you will tell me,
I would believe you.
It wouldn't matter that I know you're lying!
You lied to me so many times
and I admit,
nothing pleased me more
than your beautiful lies.
I knew you were lying.
Innocent?
What it's like now,
if I don't have anyone to talk to anymore,
if no one lies to me anymore
and I'm cold in my soul,
is better?
This year, spring is late.
You told me last year
that it's because of the polar caps melting.
It was, perhaps, one of your lies.
But now, why am I cold in April?

Lightning at the end of the world

A flyover Alaska

Gray hat
on the top of the frozen mountain,
the last breath from the toothless mouth
of a dying older man.
A century of ashes
inspired by the lung of the gray glacier.
Unfaithful witness of eternity,
from my one-moment flight,
I see a long history.
What will it be?
I'm just a flash at the end of the world.
I can't confess.

Lina

God, how much I loved Lina!
She lived far away, up on the hill,
a gypsy much older than my mother,
but she told me the most beautiful stories
of courage, love, sacrifice, and honor.
The handsome boy was always
a blue-eyed boy by my name.
"Which one do you love, dear?"
"Well, Lino, Lenuta, you know!"
I was so ashamed!
She asked me the same thing every night.
I always answered her the same way.
- Good dear, good!
But also Niculaie, how much he loved Lina!
Just her, just her,
even if "snippy snake-like enemies
wanted to take him, my dear,
 to take him from me!"
The handsome boy with my name
was not afraid to walk through the woods at night.
It went through fire and water
to save his bride
from the arms of the "red" emperor.
- Lina, but why did the dragon have eyes of fire?
- Well, my darling,
to burn the Handsome Boy.
 -Well, let him be sinful!"
When Lina has gone,
Nicolai got me on his knees;
his pants were torn

and he told me
I was growing up, that I'm big now,
that Lina sees me from above.
-          Yes, I know.
 She told me earlier
that one day she will rise in the sun!
"I don't know how to tell you stories."
"You can't, Niculaie!
You have the voice of the hoarse dragon
who ruled over the kingdom from sunrise.
Lina told me that one rainy night.

„Little boy"

I find the quiet of the evenings
in a cup of tea.
I manage to forgive myself
for the pits I stepped through.
Next to me is the book
with pages as if torn from my soul.
I forgot to return it on time.
I wish I had written it myself!
Old clock,
witness of my hesitations, is dumb.
In vain do I count my steps
with the latest type of pedometer,
not even metabolized calories
I can't calculate!
Ever since I sent you the bouquet,
no answer.
Likewise, in high school,
I wrote to the physics teacher:
"I would run with you anywhere,
even on another continent. "
I haven't told you about that before.
Of shame, of fear?
I waited in vain for a week.
She also called me "Little boy."
It was burning in her green eyes
an ironic diode;
but she did not leave me corrected.
I hear the rain trotting on the terrace.
"Maybe with tomorrow's mail;
but no, it's Sunday. "

The TV is muted,
it sits next to me stoically.
From the ceiling,
covered with "Calcio Vecchio"
a shadow descends;
an angel with green eyes.
Impertinently, she calls me "Little Boy,"
and wryly smiles.

Live rhythms

Drum beat, infinitely repeated rap,
shakes me from my dream,
wakes me up,
like the hiss of train wheels,
like the whispers of your heart
reflected in my palm,
concave mirror.
It's like being immersed in a sound bath,
It's like rubbing my skin with a sponge
pulsing in the rhythm of your heart.
Poor dream!
In a life where we fight,
regardless of wars,
of the armistices broken at any time,
with anyone, with me, with you,
hormones, vitamins, poison, enzymes.
Rhythms keep life.
We would go out silent
without the lively rhythms:
drum beat,
the rhythm of the train wheels at night,
your heartbeat
reflected in my palm,
concave mirror.

Loneliness

If you are left alone,
do not close the gate.
A weary passerby will pass,
will knock, will enter,
or who knows
will go on;
it may even be fate.
Mornings will take revenge:
you will wake up every day
with loneliness,
always the same, sister with death.
The sun will not smile on you in the window,
neither will the stars go down
to calm you down at night
when it is dark in the soul,
around.
Leave the gate open.
One day loneliness will go away;
willingly,
or maybe you'll drive it away.
Don't close the gate!

Looking West

I'm sitting on the balcony,
on the green carpet like an alfalfa field.
I look at the ocean, the blue mirror.
The sun, lazy dog,
sticks its tongue out to the West.
Reddish-yellow rays are reflected
on the surface of the water;
They arrive as if invigorated,
in my half-open eyes.
Next to me, the grill lid is cold now.
On the right, the glass with "Margarita,"
prepared with "Patron" tequila.
My recipe differs from the original:
Instead of a third tequila
and the rest, lemon juice,
I use the juice, a drop or two,
just as a pretext,
and the rest, the poison of the green devils
from the south of Rio Grande.
Well, Transylvanian reminiscences!
From "off," a warm, worried voice:
"My dear, put on your straw hat.
It's still sunny, and notice,
you are at the fourth glass. "
From the West, the distance gives birth
of long-haul planes
every quarter of a minute.
In the evening sun,
the symbol of the airlines
shines on the wings of silver birds.

Get off at International Airport.
I sat down for two minutes,
on the rocking chair.
When I woke up, it was cold.
On the table, the glass,
lily corolla open to the sky,
was empty;
was lonely, sad.

Marine

She woke up in the morning.
Lark before the wedding,
was beginning to sing.
The dawn was hiding in her locks,
melted in the waters
of the caresses of the night.
Why are you waking up frowning?
Scrape the scales off your eyelids.
Look at me like at your mother,
like your old daughter
from afar,
and sing, and laugh.
From the thick cables
salt poisoned water
flowed white, bitter.
Silence foreshadows death.
In the afternoon, she entered the sea.
She never came back
for the evening prayer.

Maternal propulsions

Every year on the second Sunday in May in the USA,
Mother's Day is celebrated.
Not "Women's Day" in general, but Mother's Day; of those
women who brought new life using the grace
the Creator gave. It is a moment of more profound meditation
on humans and their destiny.
We were all children once. We were nourished, protected,
educated, and propelled into life by a mother.
By different methods, they are deriving from the nature of
each mother, from the heart of each child, but with the same
desire to ensure success in the life of their children.
I dedicate this poem-essay to the two women who watched
over my first steps in life and determined my future like good
fairies, different but just as well-intentioned and devoted.

Propulsive charges

Where did my mother's eyes hide?
They flew too far, they fell too deep.
More painful than ever,
now I miss them the most.
Rarely did I look her straight in the eyes.
A brake of fear stopped me
before we met.
She would always blame me for something;
with a heavy voice, his eyes on fire.
Heavy voice of love,
eyes inflamed with ambition,
of devotion and hope.
"You're not fighting enough, boy!

You don't read enough,
you waste your time with trifles, and life is hard.
The laziness of the morning
will make you lose in your life;
all the mobsters will take it in front of you. "
It was her way of pushing me forward,
blaming me.
Every time,
from the wound produced, healing is born,
with the force of the vaccine
who overcomes disease through disease.
The history of the persecuted for centuries
of an arrogant and hostile world nation,
it has passed through the consciousness of generations
like a spear reddened in the fire of suffering,
generated the ambitions of the families
for the performance of the offspring,
as an act of revenge on fate.
My mother's eyes flew so far; they fell so deep!
I need her reproaches bursting not only from her words,
but also, from her stern eyes.
Now that I'm getting slower and slower,
when I bend down harder and harder,
I would need her strength to transmit
her ambitions and pride to those who came after us,
to those who have to go so far,
they have to fly so high!
I miss my mother so much!

Engineers and drivers

You can't aspire to the propulsion to success, blaming some people, especially children, for their failures, losses, reproaching their attitudes, slowness, or even unfavorable circumstances. Their sensitivities are exacerbated, their internal resources instinctively shrink, and they can't refuse to go further.

They develop a sadistic pleasure in tasting failure, an attitude of frond that can throw them astray for the rest of their lives.

Aunt Anica, my mother's sister, a monument of native peasant wisdom, warm, maternal feminine wisdom, took life as it was. She didn't make a tragedy out of failure; instead, due to the lack of brilliant successes.

Not just any lack of outstanding performance; it is a failure.

The fact that we, her grandchildren, the first four brothers, became engineers and her first four sons, our cousins, raised together, became drivers, was acceptable to her; it made her happy, proud of her and us all at the same time.

During the holidays, at family reunions, while my mother blamed us for not being ambitious enough, for not yet becoming directors or ministers in our fields of activity, Aunt Anica looked at all eight of us with pride and satisfaction, solemnly declaring:

"I'm so proud of our engineers and drivers!" Her husband, Uncle Petre, dominated by the kindness, satisfaction, and light that shone in our aunt's eyes, just nodded silently, enjoying life.

Praise and rewards from aunt Anica, a pie filled with sweet cheese and dill, sprinkled with plenty of thick sauer cream, a glass of cold "sour milk" on hot summer days, a light pat on the shoulder, or even a kiss on the scalp, always a good word,

even for small successes, often insignificant or even
unnecessary, did not compel me less than the reproaches of
my mother's harsh words and harsh looks.

Another way of looking at life; is with reasonable ambitions,
with the science of obtaining joy from small successes, even
accidental failures, from everyday life, generating powerful
impulses and propulsions.

Two sisters, two mothers, and two different women have
deeply marked my life!

I was propelled like an aircraft with two engines: one with
nuclear energy, through explosions and continuous pressure,
and the other with the turbine of a hydropower plant located
under a short dam, behind which a large lake does its job
quietly.

Medicines from Paris
(Doru)

Nothing could be hidden anymore;
I was dying of shame.
The pain in my mother's belly,
from winter vacation, made eyes;
green eyes and blond hair;
he was my little brother.
"Okay, Coane,
tomorrow, the day after tomorrow,
they'll take you to the army,
and your mother, another baby!"
Colleagues laughed,
and girl colleagues looked at me curiously.
I was angrier
than the storm of that May afternoon.
Cornelia kept pushing me:
Let's go for a walk on Vine Hill on Sunday,
but I wanted better to go to church to confess;
it seemed so great a sin to me!
Mother heroine!
You were proud to have a dream come true.
"Look, this handsome guy will take care of us!",
Dad teased me with my little brother in his arms.
„You've been gone far away, a long time."
Yesterday I received a package of medicines
from Paris.

Mind-changing

The southerly breeze washes night's hours,
breaks the time into shards with blunt edges,
fills the streets with doubt.
Ghosts hide in the gate hinges
and shout with voices choked by fear.
The lantern pole sways like a mind-changing;
Of fear, the light forgot to descend.
Two flashes rise from the highway;
the darkness seeps into the canals,
scared and defeated.
In your window, entrance to Heaven,
the same sleepy cat is waiting for me
with her blue tile eyes.
Vigilant guardian,
she stabs me with a rebellious look.
Who are you hiding from,
who are you afraid of?
By the dark, by the southerly breeze?
The night is in you.
I'm just the lantern pole
from which the light forgot to descend.
I'm waiting in the street,
swaying like a mind-changing.

Missed wedding

The monstrous coalition

I won't call you to my wedding.
Your soles
won't soil my floor.
I pray on my knees
to sprout the knots in the bed,
to make a crown
of leafy oak branches
for my bride.
Meantime, my grandma hid
between the planks.
"Even if you pass me by," she said,
you won't take Pasula's stupid girl!
They cannot even look at the sky,
to say what month we are in,
but to plow, to sow!"
The wedding has been postponed.
Eventually, it never happened.

Missing

The time of the days when I do nothing
I subtract it from the lifetime;
I add it to the time of death.
The sky is walking its stars over me.
Ghost ready to disappear,
It doesn't mind me,
it looks at me like a stone
softened in the bed of time
that's flowing slow.
Accountant of eternity,
I'm not going to try to figure out the books.
I'll smile at the damage, absent.
The time of the days when I do nothing
I subtract it from my lifetime,
I add it to the time of death.
And life goes down.
Death does not ask me;
shut up and come faster.
From the first morning
when the sun will never rise
for me,
the seconds will remain in my debt,
and duty will never return.
Accountant of eternity, correct,
I'm not going to try to figure out the books.
I'll smile at the damage, absent.

Mother 2

Mom, my heaven!
From the garden of your arms
I pick flowers in the mornings.
Some feed me, to let me grow;
others sting me to wake me up.
You caress my soul
with the mysteries of heaven
gathered in the petals of your eyes.

Mom, my cradle,
I need you.
I'm looking for you,
that of the days when you counted my steps,
when you lit up my good times,
you spread gentleness over the bad days.

When everyone forgets you,
enemies and friends,
when you'll become just a shadow
in the memories of those who will remain,
you are the cradle I want to return to,
the nest where I would like to die.
To descend in your arms of air,
to fall asleep in your arms of flowers.

My sandals got small.

I would climb into the mulberry tree even now,
but my sandals got small.
In the meantime, my beard has grown,
my face is unrecognizable.
"Don't go up in the tree, you cad,
that you'll soil the tiles around the fountain,
and your dad wouldn't have
the guts of money to pay me back,
not in a thousand years!"
The neighbor was ugly and sour.
My mother put a clean shirt on me.
"Go to church, baby,
be lucky, and be good.
Don't spoil it with mulberry again!"

The fountain has dried up,
I'm getting sadder,
Grandpa went to the cemetery on the hill.
Dad plated it with the fountains' tiles.
The neighbors' mulberry tree has dried up.
Without him, their yard is deserted.
The small sandals I never found.

Not rainwater, nor seas water

I sometimes feel, I sense,
that the springs are drying up.
I'm afraid I won't be able to supply
thirsty, innocent flocks,
and your eyes will not laugh
under the like the sky clear drops.
I'm starting to search
I run after water.
Not rainwater!
She gathers dust, shit,
washed from the long roads
which it lowered
from heaven to earth.
Nor the seas' water!
In it, gather the creatures
that no longer have a place in the deserts.
I'm looking for spring water
in which the sun returns from the night
to start his morning stories
with the first rays
reflected in your agate eyes.

November laughs with his gray teeth

Our summer wanderings,
chains of days, months,
melt, retreat,
gray clouds
crochet in a dull sky.
They go tired
with gnawed horseshoes,
with plucked feathers,
poor shadows
of the eagles that were.
It's autumn,
November laughs with his gray teeth.
Brutal, without apologizing,
hoarfrost with ice eyes
secretly sits on the leaves at night,
decorate my juniper with a silver mustache.
The whole forest froze with fear.
Defoliated, embarrassed by nakedness,
worthy, accept the sentence.
The forests remain deserted again.
November laughs with his gray teeth.

October

Autumn, through October,

I was sitting on my boulder
polished by the waters, by time.
I was throwing pebbles into a pit,
counting the burned thoughts of summer.
Nearby, a gray ghost,
the cow, was grazing quietly.
From above, from the forest,
was lowering the rustling of the leaves;
they lived, sadly,
the last days before the fall.
Lazy white smoke rose
from Father Philip's court,
rotating in spirals.
In the summer kitchen
they were boiling the jam of plum.
I was thinking about Helen,
at her green eyes,
at the heavy chestnut from her locks.

Old silver

The sad charm of twilight

It is too late to polish the silverware,
and I'm not in the mood .....
Each piece evokes painful memories;
I would like to forget some of them.
The decorated with flowers teapot,
father brought it from Russia
wrapped in an astrakhan fur hat
when he returned from the war.
The cutlery forgot by the Germans
when they left in a hurry,
driven away by people of cold,
and came down from distant Siberia.
Curious children,
we were looking at the treasures with wide eyes.
They barely escaped being confiscated
by the militia at their searches in the fifties.
My engagement bow tie needle
and your bride's crown are crooked.
The silver wasn't good quality,
you remember, we bought what we found,
poor mindless and homeless young people.
Parent's silver wedding ring I'll keep;
I'll look at them sadly sometimes.
You are not with me anymore,
to caress them with silent eyes,
to shake our heads lazily ...
What time is it?
It's like I fell asleep a little.
I'm leaving them now,
but I'll be doing them tomorrow!

Dan C David

Olive face

I don't understand what's going on in class.
The sun doesn't seem to enter the same window;
it doesn't fall the same way on your olive face.
You don't even look at me anymore, sims!
Not even on the sly,
like yesterday, before the crazy run.
We stopped by the river
with the name stolen from the emperor's daughter.
I undressed in broad daylight.
You hid in the bushes,
 ashamed as the first woman
from the garden of the first sin.
Sharp stones, and broken branches,
pricked our arms, our ribs,
and your white thighs were scratched.
A deserted silence buried us.
Not even the warm evening sun
failed to lift us.
Today it seems as if the sun
is no longer falling the same way
on your olive face.

Ongoing

If we could fly like birds,

and we would meet by accident
somewhere under the clouds of our winters,
I would say hello to you,
like to any stranger;
we wouldn't know each other.
You're not going to wear
the same hat again,
the same sour cherry cloak,
the same flower looks,
from long ago.
I'll have a cane from a walnut branch,
and a sad smile;
you won't remember it.
It will be crippled,
it will have wrinkles,
and a beard like battered snow.
In my heart, just, maybe,
I will feel a flash,
ordered from somewhere indefinitely,
and I will look back, unconscious.
Perhaps you'll feel a chill too,
and you will think:
It is, of course, by the draught.

Only the sky
(C V David - 111)

Don't cover me with earth!
I'm going to be cold.
I'm afraid of poisoning
with the sadness of my blood
the innocent living things,
committing even more sins.
Someday I'll be called.
I'll have to get up.
Unbreakable frame,
the dry clay will stop me.
I will weep in the ground
with murky streams.
The springs will no longer be usable;
their water will be bitter and salty.
Better keep me in your minds;
leave me the sky as the roof,
to be able to see the stars at night,
angels at day,
you, when you'll sprinkle a thought on me.
Memories will line up, blue flowers
on the plain where I will sleep.
Some kids I won't know
will gather them, will adorn themself.
When the trumpets will sound,
I'll wake up.
Don't cover me with earth!
I'm going to be cold.

Our love, a jumble, a mess
Quadrilogs

In the semi-dark room,
the vibrations of our hearts
bump into walls,
interferes.
The result is a jumble, a mess.
The windows are shaking,
the chandelier with the lamps off
oscillates platonic
next to the tuberose bouquet
fallen out of the vase.
We love each other, you see,
but the echo, the walls, and the corners,
distort our words, facts, thoughts,
they quadrilog in a polyphonic choir,
each after another score.
Nothing is understood anymore.
The result is a jumble, a mess.

Out of the limits

I don't want to stay in this room

anymore.
We get bored
like two pears left on the shelf
to ripen.
Morning, day, ... still going,
but in the evening
I can no longer bear it;
They crumble all over me.
I'd like to take you by the neck,
so, as at school,
and let's go where we can see,
to have fun, let's try,
to succeed, maybe!
Too bad.
You're only with the soul
in my mind!
I'd like to take you by the neck,
so, as a school,
and let's go where we can see.

Panicked

Hawk in the summer sky,
I'm looking for you
floating alone;
I revolve around my thought.
I feel like an electron
caressed by the light.
Why can't I remember
the words I made ready for a week?
The balance of the horizon tilts.
I'm panicking, dizzy.
Why can't I remember
the words I made ready for a week?
What can I tell you
when we will meet?

Paraschiva sent me for a walk

I walk at random;
I don't care anymore
about the intersections,
about pedestrian crossings,
or traffic lights.
I'm sad; I have no purpose.
Paraschiva sent me for a walk.
Two stray dogs are following me;
they hope to receive something;
a piece of bread, maybe?
At least they have a clear purpose.
Two middle-aged ladies
look at me in amazement
shaking their glasses
like two hens at dusk.
What else do they want?
A guy as big as the college pole
come across me by chance,
almost overthrowing me.
I am going further.
I'm sad, I have no purpose.
Paraschiva sent me for a walk.

Past

It's been so long
since I've been trying to forget you!
Days and years are no longer a measure;
it needs a miracle,
an abyss into which to fall,
in which to dive.
Bird without a nest, bear without den,
maze-free snake,
alone in a world I can't get out of,
which I can't understand,
I tried tequila;
it did not fit!
My prayers were not answered either.
I'm afraid of sleepless nights,
of sick mornings,
faces of the same senseless time.
My space tightens around my forehead
like that in an ready to explode atom,
to throw sadness and longing,
to abandon them in the middle of the road,
in the wake of the past;
Old clothes, torn clothes ... past.

Philosophy and mineral water

I sit in the kitchen, talking to myself
in front of a mineral water bottle.
Marital crises
start for very different reasons,
not just from disobedient children.
Character mismatches
or sexual disharmony
are rarer than quarrels
between the two "grandmothers."
Something changes every day.
Often the dynamics of life
take precedence over us
and we barely crawl, limping,
panting behind them.
The climate on Earth does not change that way
as reported on the news channels,
or at international conferences.
Talkative, confident, closed to dialogue,
gather to talk,
to drink coffee with soy milk
and with synthetic sweeteners instead of caster sugar.
Cinemas have emigrated in masse
from the "high street" through the apartments in the block,
and give rise to conflicts
that have never existed before.
I spend more time in the kitchen.
I'm talking to myself in front of a bottle of Bodoc.

You're trapped over the head
in the last episode of the soap opera
with the poor girl and with the boy

who stumbled into luck.
What's left
from the harmony of our married life?
Our neighbors were lurking behind the curtains; they gave us
the example to their flying sons-in-law,
late married grandchildren
and even the rebellious daughters-in-law!
I let the mineral water breathe into the glass.
I'm going to bed.

Potentially perfect

You are the potentially perfect woman.
If you had a talent for painting,
you would have been an elite painter.
If you could sing,
you would have been an eminent musician.
You would have been a matchless mistress
if you knew how to love
So, you're just the woman
who does not paint,
who does not sing.
Who loves
how she washes the laundry,
how she cooks
how she raises her children;
with soul, with a good feeling.
An almost perfect woman.

Reapers

The reapers of the plain are gone.
I'm surrounded by the autumn,
to ruin my silence.
Black beads,
the crows lined on the stubble.
Here and there, yellow beams and ears.
Old thoughts sting me underfoot,
and the stubble is now deserted.
The lightning bolts also went out.
Will they come back next year?
Who knows?
They took their summer loves with them.
Because they long, the light of summer dies.
We can't find poppies on the stubble.
In their absence, the solitude defeated us.
The stories with beautiful guys
living a whole life in an instant,
they went away in memory;
they all passed into dreams.

The reapers of the plain are gone,
blue-flowered eyes, with golden hair,
eternal monuments of pride.
Will they come back next year?
Who knows?
You went through childhood,
you don't come back.

Rest on the rock

No sound,
no rustling behind you,
no breeze.
Your steps seem to slip.
I was expecting at least one hiss
of a serpent crawling through the sand,
at least a flutter of a broken wing.
Nothing!
Light prey,
I got into the cunning game,
and I never went out again.
It was a hidden signal.
It was a wonder.
Was it a mystery?
No, it wasn't love!
When I woke up,
a brown eagle swayed
with a snake in its claws.
The night came down calmly
like an astonishment.

Running

I ended up panting at the first oak.
You were lagging.
The green eyes of trees
 were crying for mercy
with heavy chlorophyll tears.
Sighing, they looked at me
like a horse eating embers.
Late, you're here;
You fell into my arms.
The rustle of the forest peace.
Only then
I made peace with the leaves.
They were laughing, laughing,
green eyes,
dew tears
looking towards the sun.
Dazzling, it had risen.
The morning hid upset.
The day was now
just ours.

Sleep

The stars have no peace, glistening all night.
They send me messages
encoded in traveling photons.
I decipher it instantly
as if I knew them before they were issued.
It's like I whispered them,
and they return to me.
Old Morse, for a while,
stopped listening to our stories;
the messages are getting sadder.
The enigmatic guy cuts off indecent words,
I love you; I want you, I dream of you,
I am waiting for you.
Escape only the agonies of the climate,
autumn's cold frowns, and curses of severe winters.
Your messages are getting dimmer every day;
I almost don't feel them lately.
The distance between us has increased,
or the gray forgetfulness sort hem carelessly
and throws them in its trash,
where do they all end up at once?
The dawn is coming; the sky washes its cheek,
and the tired stars descend silently in their sleep.
I pull the shutters over the stillness of my thoughts.
Everything is erased, everything disappears,
I fall asleep.

Stars

From up on the block,
I look at the stars like a hen; with one eye.
That way, the poor stars
don't tremble anymore in interstellar frost
in which they are born, evolve, and die.
You feel like I'm out for smoking.
But do you think I can, when far away,
so close, above my eyes,
in the interstellar frost, those hearts of light
are born, evolve, and die?
Right now, when you take off your dressing gown,
and you're getting ready for bed
among the colored plastic curlers,
in a sea of toothpaste, mouthwash,
in the interstellar cold, those little monsters
with the eyes of a child, are born, evolve, and die.
From up here, I can see beyond the boutique
from the locomotive depot,
the one I buy from time to time,
when we hurry, a bottle of whiskey
and a box of condoms.
Poor Nicoleta, who reads her love novels,
has no idea that somewhere,
in the interstellar frost,
those glittering dwarfs
are born, evolve, and die!

The beginning of the end

By fear, despair,
I smoked cigarette after cigarette.
You were sitting on the edge of the bed
with your head in your hands,
bent by thoughts, by doubt.
What happened to us?
I didn't know where to start,
how far to go.
The lamp with enameled tin shade,
went out.
We had no more between us
not even that dust of light
who had vibrated for so long,
anemic, ready to die.
We didn't see each other.
The air in the room
had become unbreathable;
of your thoughts,
of your doubts.
I felt like a hunted animal.
Among the thin blinds,
morning returned lazily.
Sleep never came.

The comb

I see you in the fog;
shadow wrapped in white sheets,
ghost in the winter's holidays.
The lines of the body
are barely distinguishable.
You see me the same way, I guess.
What can two ghosts say to each other?
All memories are gone.
I see your comb.
You don't need it anymore.
Once you have arranged your hair,
melt gold waterfall with it.
I was trying to figure out
 if you were awake.
Your deep eyes filled with tears.
Old doctor
bald as an apple kept in the hay,
 answers me in a hurry:
"We're trying, sir, we're trying,
all is not lost yet. "
How can you sleep, My Lord,
when is her heart so sick?

The depot

Today is a good time;
It is not cold; it's either not too hot.
A flock of crows falls from the forest
on the plums left by the leaves.
From the top of the stairs to the square
I see the old depot beyond the railway;
a sore wound,
and I feel it going up,
I don't even know where from,
from mind to mind, the sadness like a mist.

...... The moon hadn't appeared yet ....
I walked on the rails,
whistling a little fake
for fear of savage packs of dogs.
I don't know why it made me cry.
I was waiting for you under the clock
on our bench, at the panel.
Prisoners of frustration,
my colleagues avoided looking at me.
You never came.
The brakeman whispered bitterly to me:
"She fell between the rails in the depot."

The hill in flames

In the evening light

the sun sacrifices the day,
the lamb of the forgiveness of his sins.
From the brink of the horizon
blood waves are coming down,
the sacrifice of the day that is going out;
cherry wine
for the late feast.
Devoted photons,
soldiers of the queen of light,
sacrifice their lives without a murmur.
It's a hot rush,
the aftermath of colossal events,
epitaph in red on the crypt of the day
which bows its torn flag.
Biased witness,
my red hill closes its eyes
and sleeps with me.
It doesn't see the moment
in which the day goes out.
You forgave me.

Killed by Parkinson owl

I turned my gaze to the screen.
It blinked like a cunning older woman's eyes.

I stuck my fingers on the keyboard,
black as midnight.
I muttered in my beard.
  "No, I don't want to listen to you anymore!"
I was building arguments in my mind,
word chains, impenetrable nets,
to convince you that you are wrong.
  "Go to bed, dear!
Stay like an owl all night on the keys
with Parkinson's rebellious fingers
and with half-blind eyes,
dipped in the blue
of the monster with the diode screen.
I'll find you dead one morning.
I don't even know how to stop it. "
I argued with you, in my mind, until late.
I didn't realize when you've shut up.
I looked at you like a whimsical angel.
You're still a child!
I try to give you a light caress
but my hands are shaking.
You sleep frowning, tight as a pretzel.
Would you be right!?
I realized it got cold.

The pillow

I don't mind the pillow
that sleeps between us

like a crumpled hat;
it collects our sweat on warm nights,
and it smells like us.
It leans your back, so you don't get in pain
when you forget about yourself
and sleep on your right.
As you feel the warm pillow on your back,
sleep is coming, called by pheromones
who have undergone genetic mutations
and they reversed their purpose.
Sometimes when I wake up
from troubled dreams, and I miss you,
I feel like catching the pillow
and throw it out the window.
The sleepless squirrel
visiting us in the morning,
looks at us in amazement with round eyes
through the mesh screen;
it doesn't understand what's going on
and rages furiously.
Then I am ashamed;
I remember your saddle pain
when you forget about yourself
and sleep on your right.

The Queen of the Caves

In the age of ultra-fast computers,
I'm the caveman.

I wouldn't say I like
pointless phone conversations,
I wouldn't say I like
to waste my time on TV,
I wouldn't say I want to fly.
Lightning in the clouds with hostile tasks,
when you entered, the room lit up.
God, why did you punish me,
taking Jasmine out of the Himalayas?
Goddess carved from the silence of the snow,
you flutter your silk skirts
in miraculous pirouettes,
in front of my gleaming eyes.
Jasmine,
you are the Queen of the Caves to me.

The red rooster

Grandma would gather us around
in the evening.

There were many of us;
children from several mothers,
brothers, sisters, and cousins.
She was telling us the story of the red rooster.
We were falling asleep one by one.
Who stayed awake after all
were declared the most brilliant child of the family;
he would receive a large spoonful of sour cream
and a slice of white bread,
to be easier able to fall asleep.
I was always hungry for cream,
but also about Grandma's story.
I would have stayed awake
until the roosters crowded.

At bedtime, after her prayer,
grandma mumbled softly
from her bed with red linen:
"Who were you
who touched the pot with "groștior"?
I'll not be telling you
the story of the rooster anymore."

The sad charm of the twilight

I'll be back to you one night,

memories almost forgotten
in the ragged suitcase
from the dream warehouse.
You won't recognize me.
I will weep at every remembrance,
I will laugh, I will cry;
but you?
Apple trees in bloom,
good old friends now
will caress my shoulders again,
or they will be surprised
that the evenings are sad,
and time is running out,
and their flowers shook, defeated?
The hill at the top of which
I dreamed of raising a cross,
will it be balder,
will it be shorter,
will it be steeper?
Will it help me
when will I get him up again?
You won't understand either
how dusk fell between us,
and takes us by the hands,
two shades of wax.
Almost forgotten memories,
I'll be back to you, whiter, one night.

The same linden

Your best photo
I'm keeping it in the bizarre memory's album.
Among the linden's branches
poor dusk's rays
sculpt on your face
leaf tracks
like question marks.
If I've known since then,
I would have sent you with them
on another planet,
and I was looking at you from afar,
occasionally,
only through the telescope.
My life without you
would have been, of course, empty,
a lost chance,
vault left without keys,
but at least I'd have gotten rid
of the interrogations
when the poor rays of the evening
sculpt on your face,
like question marks,
the leaves of the same linden.

The sky, like a white sea

I see the mountains far away,
gray old guys
begging for mercy from heaven.
The sky paints their ridges
with white powder.
I hear their whispers
by the mist breath of morning.
They reach me
on the waters of thin streams,
rippling among the boulders
sanded by the unforgiving time brush.
In the distance,
I see the mountains,
snow-capped ridges
from the sky like a white sea.

The stranger in the mirror

We meet quite often,
we smile at each other.
Sometimes I feel like you're looking for me,
that you want to see me,
other times,
you have something to tell me
but you dare not.
Why is it hard for you?
Are my looks foreign to you?
You've been worrying me lately;
your forehead is withered,
scratched under the drizzle,
the cheek, a delta riddled by snakes,
the eyes, the folds of a dreaded ghost.
I barely recognized you;
you were dizzy,
your heavy shoulders bent your knees,
between sparse, yellow teeth,
you stammer incomprehensible words.
Or we didn't know each other,
never before?

The wine is made

The wine is made,

the soul burned by the sun.
It reached the stillness of last judgment.
Under the cold vault, 'imprisoned in the staves,
the nectar called its soldiers;
it put them in a state of war,
to defeat the best and the strongest.

The occult powers tickle essences.
The variety of liqueurs rises in degrees
from shadows, murmurs, and whispers
Slowly, slowly the wine clears;
to quench the thirst of the desert within us.

Old Zeus stingy kept
the secret of the wine only for itself,
to be a cure for the toil and sorrow,
but Bacchus, the passionate,
spread it throughout the world.
The sin remained unpunished.
After that, the man drank it.
He exclaimed happily:
„In vino veritas" and ... he was silent.

Then, barely
paparazzi

Desperate by the cruelty
of the naughty paparazzi,
by the poison of their thought,
I ran across the scorched field,
to hide you, to save you.
I absorbed you into orbit
behind the eyes,
thread by thread, piece by piece.
Invisible,
no more interest,
they abandoned you
like a veiled film.
I'm afraid to bring you back to life now,
to recompose you thread by thread,
piece by piece.
The paparazzi are not dead!
We will wait;
to forget,
to forget you.
Your eyes will not burn,
your long hair won't slip,
a river of gold over the holy shoulders.
We will show ourselves to the world then, barely;
Old people, good people.

Thirst does not pass with stum!

The clouds don't dare to descend.
"Slightly rickety" baby,
I look at them sadly,
like at an empty bag.
It hasn't rained since August,
in vain, we call it "autumn";
it is as dry as corn cobs,
ready to die.
The grapes are lucky;
they quench their thirst from deep;
at least we will have stum!
I climb the vineyard on the hill.
Next to the bent cross
I see in the distance our dusty street.
I'm thirsty in the twilight.
I also see the roof of our house.
It's like the tile is redder,
beaten by the setting sun.
No, thirst doesn't pass away with stum.

Threatening

How anxious I am in my soul,
I can't drown it
in no lake in no sea in the world.
They are all
or too shallow,
or too small.
Only you
when you touch my chest
and you're threatening me
that you'll go on,
you make me give up
to think of death.
That would be commonplace,
it's not worth wasting time.

Tie your donkey in the barn

They have gathered all the horses of the city,
they forbade them to moan.
Poor horses,
they looked with wet, puzzled eyes.
Anyway, they didn't moan too often,
not too loud;
they were barely grumbling.
The most dissatisfied were the children.
They liked to moan
while riding on broomsticks!
They did not copy;
they were moaning.
The strike that followed
raised the moan to the status of a problem.
Between the enemies and partisans,
a fierce confrontation began.
I felt a little guilty;
at night, secretly,
I would moan sometimes
accompanied by a guitar:
"Tie your donkey in the barn."

Tired sun

Desert intersection.
We haven't met.
You go ahead,
I always keep my right hand;
I'm coming back from where I started.
You are no longer.
From afar,
the ocean sends me
the reflection of a tired sun.
You always go ahead,
Further and further.
No chance of meeting
each other.

Train station's footbridge

Packed in ages' diapers,
I didn't notice around
the roads I was carried on by hostile times.
Now, I'm sitting
on the train station's footbridge,
where I first woke up;
the memory of my mother
holding her by the lap.
I grabbed the innocent tick
to suck my finger in my toothless mouth.
I repeat the last itinerary:
A locomotive returns
to the long-abandoned depot.
She's not with me anymore,
to hold my hand, to command me:
Be good baby, be careful not to fall!
I look down to the streets that are no more,
they were torn down, moved;
They only remained in my memory
locked in the "then" position.
Just the train station, the little relic
which I love as it is, cries when it rains,
sheltering travelers under its eaves,
still broken.
Come on, mom's dear, wake up,
you have to go to school!

Under the willows

We walk under the willows.
At Iepuraşului stream,
it's shade; it's cool.
I'm silent; you're not.
Spring is upon us
through willow buds.
I know that; you may not.
Sunburned,
bee has gone astray in your hair;
it spreads pollen among your threads.
She was attracted to what attracted me too:
a perfume like honey.
You look at me with the eyes of a child
for which life is a funny story.
I look at you with the eyes of a monk
pushed by the devil into sin.
I know that, you don't.
Do you not?
You smile with meaning;
What do you know and I don't?
- You know, spring is upon us
through willow buds.
-Yes? So it seems to me.

Waves in the Pacific

Hawaii

Waves,
blue tears.
Waves,
running foams
pushed by the eyes of the young wind.
Waves,
and thoughts are falling asleep.
In the morning,
poor dreams,
they break the shores with whispered beaches.
They no longer see
the sharpened eyes of the sharks,
stabbed black arrows
in the blue soul of the warm waters.
Coming waves,
passing waves,
leaving waves.
We.

What time is it?

You think you could leave like this,
pure and simple,
taking your yellow suitcase,
(it always made me crazy)
and leave?
Not! You will stay!
The ducks
from the trenches of the neighbors
would quack at me,
the dogs from the unfenced yards,
would bark at me.
Even Fane the postman
with a crooked mouth,
like a waystation
from which the travelers departed
with the last train,
would laugh at me.
Not!
You will stay!
I need a person
which I ask every morning:
What time is it?

What would they have found at sea?

Twilight spreads its golden sheets to dry.
During the day,
untied torpors
borrowed lascivious waves,
metallic reflections,
and they sold cheap themself,
unscrupulously, to the wind,
which was passing
impassive
over thirsty beaches.
A cloud as thin as a sluggish thought
shadows the chalk face of the evening sky;
passes by, stiff, uncompromising,
turkey refused
by a pretentious partner.
What would they have found at sea, dear?
It doesn't compare to the fairies of the evening
in the solitude of "Piatra Arsă"!

Whimsical little girl

The blade of grass tastes the heaven
with its green tongue.
Salivates; are good.
The sun has not yet risen,
the dew has not dried.
The bees sleep lazily
until noon.
From the South,
the Baia Mare race passes silently;
black hawk gliding across the sky.
Dad sharpens his scythe
in the shade of the willow.
He looks straight ahead
with a frown,
threatening like an executioner.
He does not care.
I feel sorry for so many severed lives;
I want to run to my mother,
at home, to tell her.
"Hey, you're a big boy now;
stop crying like a whimsical little girl!"

Why don't you knock on my gate again?

When you pass my house

why don't you call,
why don't you knock on my gate again,
like before?
You know I'm waiting for you.
The gate would open on its own,
the chandelier would suddenly wake up,
the light would dazzle again,
to receive you.

You're bored

You stay in the back of the window

like a cat
locked in a house with no rats.
You're bored.
The view, a deep lake;
on his mirror,
no mosquito buzzing.
Enchanted evening.
I know you're thinking of me.
You're not too far from me either.
You saw me.
A shock went through my chest.
The electromagnet
received high voltage.
I flew,
pushed by the soul only,
through the window.
You looked at me in amazement.
I was a ghost
who inexplicably appeared in the house.
You're bored today.
You'll get over it!

You never left

I didn't expect the world to change suddenly.

How to make grapes ripen in one day?
Maybe just the flowers to fade!
Things are slowly changing
in our lives.
Days are alike, boredom, gray hours,
the nights are repeated,
often with the same dreams,
with the same indecisions.
When you came, or when you came down,
I don't even know how to call it,
I don't even remember,
it was like a surprise at dawn;
as if the sun had risen
right in the middle of a quiet night.
Surprised by the white
in which my heart sank
without warning me,
without telling me,
I covered my eyes with my palms.
I'm resurrected.
I didn't expect the world to change suddenly.
You never left.

You want red, you want bright

Eh, now I know;

I should have lured you differently.
Doesn't go anymore with a pair of jeans,
with a Turkish lipstick;
these were then, after the revolution.
Now it comes with a cell phone,
delicate thighs, video cameras, and giant plasmas.
It's not for me!
Why has the world become so petty?
I proposed to you a haircut worthy of a bride;
something new, original method,
stainless steel color with tourmaline reflections.
I wouldn't succeed with any other woman
to style her so carefully.
You, no, and no; that it's not in trend,
that you want red, that you wish to bright,
and a lock of hair,
something fiery, to fit the new car.
You are no longer the innocent soul,
the being I would have been able to sell hair clippers,
scissors, combs, everything.
Even to become a monk would have been acceptable.
You're no longer the little girl with the tails.
Birds scared by the surrounding storm,
we flew wherever we could.
We have failed in different worlds.

Your brass hair

From behind,

furry bear with green fur,
the mountain covers us with shadows.
Step by step after us,
he crawls, panting.
Diffuse pain, invisible knife,
his breath is frozen.
Penetrates in slowly.
At the foot of the green mountain,
white sand like a veil
on the face of a bride.
Brown camel with two humps,
your bra's traces
defies the grim shadow.
From somewhere far away
the lying sun stumbles
lost in your brass hair.

Your train has left

From the crowded train station,

like a mound, like a city,
the trains leave in silence.
Manipulated from the shadows,
the colors change muted.
No beep
disturbs the sad silence.
Just a whisper, maybe,
in the locomotive driver's helmet.
Who knows how many trains
went, where?
I'm returning home thinking of you.
Your train has left.
Without me.

Bio-bibliographic sequences

-I was born on September 9, 1936, in Leleiu, Sălaj, Romania.
-1956-1962 Faculty of Chemistry (Bucharest Polytechnic Institute).
-1954-1996 I worked at Copşa Mică, Oneşti, Piteşti, Midia-Năvodari, Bucharest, in Romania.
-1997, after retirement, I emigrated to the USA.
I worked at the University of California, Los Angeles.
-In Romania, I published between 1972 and 1974
technical books and scientific education books for children, together with Dr. eng. Victor Laiber, at the Technical Publishing House and the Ion Creangă Publishing House.
-In the USA, I published 32 volumes of poetry
in Romanian, three in English, and three volumes
of prose in Romanian.
-In the USA, I published poetry in Clipa Magazine in Los Angeles, in Origini-Romanian Roots Magazine, and several online publications on the internet:
Respiro Magazine, Agonia Magazine, Timpul Magazine, Now Magazine, Literary Network, Bocancul Literar Magazine, ITACA Magazine in Dublin, "Sălajul pur şi simply" Magazine, "Parnas 2 Magazine", Singur Magazine.
-Being in the USA, I was published in 14 volumes of poetry anthologies from Romania and the USA:
-In the USA, I published poetry and prose in my weblog on the Wordpress.com portal (https://dandavid.wordpress.com), on my page on the Facebook Social Network (https://www.facebook.com/ dan.david.332), and the "Love, Wounding Blood" and "Alone" pages on Facebook.

Table of content

32	Heavy sadness	43
33	Horses with red hooves	44
34	I don't want to play anymore!	45
35	I don't care!	46
36	I feel you that you feel like me	47
37	I'm dreaming of a different kind of fall	48
38	I'm hoping like a frog	49
39	I rise from the sand	50
40	I will smile at you	51
41	Insidious memories	52
42	Irregular clocks	53
43	It's just a profession	55
44	It would simplify everything	56
45	Jellyfish in love	57
46	Just as I get closer to you	58
47	Late spring	59
48	Lightning at the end of the world	60
49	Lina	61
50	"Little boy"	63
51	Live rhythms	65
52	Loneliness	66
53	Looking West	67
54	Marine	69
55	Maternal propulsions	70
56	Medicines from Paris	74
57	Mind changing	75
58	Missed wedding	76
59	Missing	77
60	Mother 2	78
61	My sandals got small	79
62	Not rainwater, nor seas water	80
63	November laughs with his gray teeth	81
64	October	82

65	Old silver	83
66	Olive face	84
67	Ongoing	85
68	Only the sky	86
69	Our love, a jumble, a mess	87
70	Out of the limits	88
71	Panicked	89
72	Paraschiva sent me for a wal	90
73	Past	91
74	Philosophy and mineral water	92
75	Potentially perfect	94
76	Reapers	95
77	Rest on the rock	96
78	Running	97
79	Sleep	98
80	Stars	99
81	The beginning of the end	100
82	The comb	101
83	The depot	102
84	The hill in flames	103
85	Killed by Parkinson owl	104
86	The pillow	105
87	The Queen of the Caves	106
88	The red rooster	107
89	The sad charm of the twilight	108
90	The same linden	109
91	The sky, like a white sea	110
92	The stranger in the mirror	111
93	The wine is made	112
94	Then, barely	113
95	Thirst does not pass with stum!	114
96	Threatening	115
97	Tie your donkey in the barn	116

Made in the USA
Monee, IL
23 August 2022

2e263ecd-ce3d-4e3e-ad5d-acabc2c2611eR01